Calligraphy Meets Philosophy

Talk 1

尚語

第一話

KS Vincent POON（潘君尚）

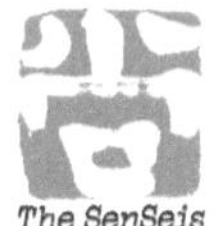

The SenSeis

First Edition
Aug 2022

Published by
The SenSeis 尚尚齋
Toronto
Canada
www.thesenseis.com
publishing@thesenseis.com

ISBN 978-1-989485-30-9

Cover
Kanazawa Shinise Memorial Hall
金澤市老舗紀念館
Kanazawa   Japan

In Loving Memory of My Beloved Mother

Pui Luen Nora TSANG（曾佩鑾）

Table of Contents

Calligraphy Meets Philosophy

Introduction

(I)

Content is the soul of an artwork.

Thus, catching the soul of Chinese calligraphy requires understanding the literary contents. To facilitate this, the *Calligraphy Meets Philosophy* series presents traditional Chinese calligraphy alongside line-by-line translated texts with remarks and footnotes.

(II)

Traditional Chinese calligraphy is not just about physical aesthetics. The art is also a reflection of one's temperament, charisma, refinement, and philosophies[1]. Literary contents scribed by calligraphers thus play a significant role in the art and should never be overlooked. Indeed, *Lanting Xu* (《蘭亭序》), the most renowned piece of calligraphy in Chinese history, is not only praised for its aesthetics but also for its literary content[2].

(III)

Calligraphy Meets Philosophy – Talk 1 (《尚語・第一話》) includes three calligraphic works and their translations: *Heart Sutra* (《般若波羅蜜多心經》), *Great Learning* (《大學》), and *Zhuangzi - The Secret of Caring for Life* (《莊子・養生主》). It also includes *Revisions to "An English Translation and the Correct Interpretation of Laozi's Tao Te Ching"*.

(IV)

This book could not have been published without the help of my father, Dr Kwok Kin POON (潘國鍵博士). I sincerely thank his priceless advice in my translations throughout the series. His unwavering support and tutelage have always been the chief drivers of my passion for learning and transmitting traditional Chinese calligraphy and culture.

Knowledge is never pursued alone.

KS Vincent Poon
August 2022, Toronto

Footnotes

(1). 梁披雲主編,《中國書法大辭典》. Guangdong: 廣東人民出版社 , 1991, p.73.

(2). KS Vincent Poon & Kwok Kin Poon, *English Translation of Classical Chinese Calligraphy Masterpieces*. Toronto: The Sen-Seis, 2019, p.43.

Heart Sutra

(《般若波羅蜜多心經》)

Calligraphy

Calligrapher (書者): KS Vincent Poon (潘君尚)

Content (內容): *Heart Sutra* (《 般若波羅蜜多心經 》)

Style (字體): Small Standard Script (小楷)

Caption (款識): 般若波羅蜜多心經潘君尚沐手敬書 (*Heart Sutra,* KS Vincent Poon scribed with due respect and cleansed hands)

Seal Inscription (鈐印): 君尚 (朱文) (Kwan Sheung, red characters), 潘氏 (白文) (The Surname of Poon, white characters)

Medium (材料): Ink on Xuan paper (紙墨水本)

Size (尺寸): 66 X 35cm

Year (年份): 2020

觀自在菩薩行深般若波羅蜜多時照見五蘊皆空度一切苦厄舍利子
色不異空空不異色色即是空空即是色受想行識亦復如是舍利子是
諸法空相不生不滅不垢不淨不增不減是故空中無色無受想行識無
眼耳鼻舌身意無色聲香味觸法無眼界乃至無意識界無無明亦無無
明盡乃至無老死亦無老死盡無苦集滅道無智亦無得以無所得故菩
提薩埵依般若波羅蜜多故心無罣礙無罣礙故無有恐怖遠離顛倒夢
想究竟涅槃三世諸佛依般若波羅蜜多故得阿耨多羅三藐三菩提故
知般若波羅蜜多是大神咒是大明咒是無上咒是無等等咒能除一切
苦真實不虛故說般若波羅蜜多咒即說咒曰揭諦揭諦波羅揭諦波羅
僧揭諦菩提薩婆訶

般若波羅蜜多心經潘君尚沐手敬書

Translation

Note: *The original Chinese and its sentence arrangement follow the 《大明太祖高皇帝御製般若心經 (Heart Sutra: An Imperial Rendition by Emperor Taizu of the Great Ming Empire) 》* [1]. *Specialized terms in Buddhism are imported from renditions by Edward Conze* [2] *and the Ven. Dharma Master Lok To (樂渡長老)* [3].

般若波羅蜜多心經
Heart Sutra

1. 觀自在菩薩，行深般若波羅蜜多時，
When the Bodhisattva Avalokiteśvara (觀自在菩薩)[4] ruminated wisely and deeply (行深)[5] to reach the state of Prajna Paramita (般若波羅蜜多, the Perfection of Transcendent Wisdom),

2. 照見五蘊皆空，度一切苦厄。
He perceived and understood (照見) that all Five Skandhas (五蘊) are of Nothingness (空)[6], and He vowed to transcend all (度一切)[7] to depart all anguishes and sufferings (苦厄).

3. 舍利子，
O Sariputra,

4. 色不異空，空不異色;
Form does not differ from Nothingness, and Nothingness does not differ from Form;

5. 色即是空，空即是色。
Form is Nothingness, and Nothingness is Form.

6. 受想行識亦復如是。
The same also applies to feelings, perceptions, volitions and consciousness (行識).

7. 舍利子，
O Sariputra,

8. 是諸法空相 , 不生不滅 ,
all dharmas (諸法) are marked with the manifestation of Nothingness, they are neither created nor destructible,

9. 不垢不淨 , 不增不減。
they cannot be defiled nor purified, they cannot be augmented
nor diminished.

10. 是故空中, 無色 , 無受想行識 ,
Hence, within Nothingness, there is no form, no feeling, no per-
ception, no volition, and no consciousness,

11. 無眼耳鼻舌身意 , 無色聲香味觸法 ,
no eye, no ear, no nose, no tongue, no body, no thoughts, no
form, no sound, no smell, no taste, no tangible objects, and no
objects from thoughts,

12. 無眼界 , 乃至無意識界。
no realm of the sense of sight and so forth, even to the extent of
no realm of consciousness.

13. 無無明 , 亦無無明盡 ,
There is no ignorance, and so no annihilation of no ignorance,

14. 乃至無老死 , 亦無老死盡。
and there is even no decay and death, and so no extinction of
decay and death.

15. 無苦集滅道 ,
There is no suffering and no origin (集) of suffering, and there is
no cessation of suffering and no path to the cessation of suffering,

16. 無智亦無得 , 以無所得故。
there is no wisdom and no attainment of anything whatsoever, for
there is nothing to be attained.

17. 菩提薩埵，依般若波羅蜜多故。
The Bodhisattva (菩提薩埵) transcends, for He follows and practises the Prajna Paramita.

18. 心無罣礙，無罣礙故。
He has no hindrance in His mind, for His mind is free of hindrance.

19. 無有恐怖，遠離顛倒夢想，究竟涅槃。
He has no fear, He stays far away from delusional dreams and ultimately reaches the state of Nirvana (涅槃).

20. 三世諸佛，依般若波羅蜜多故，得阿耨多羅三藐三菩提。
The Buddhas of the Past, Present and Future, for they follow and practise the Prajna Paramita, have attained the Supreme Enlightenment (阿耨多羅三藐三菩提).

21. 故知般若波羅蜜多，是大神咒，
Thus, know that the Prajna Paramita (Prajna Paramita Chant) is the Great Divine Spell,

22. 是大明咒，是無上咒，是無等等咒，
the Great Spell of Illumination, the Supreme Spell, and the Unequalled Spell among all,

23. 能除一切苦，眞實不虛故。
which can allay one from all suffering, for it is authentic and not spurious (眞實不虛).

24. 說般若波羅蜜多咒，卽說咒曰：
Hence, if one recites the Prajna Parmita Chant, it is then recited as:

25. 揭帝揭帝，波羅揭帝，波羅僧揭帝，菩提僧莎訶。
Gate, Gate, Paragate, Parasamgate, Bodhi Svaha.

(translated by KS Vincent Poon, Mar. 2017; revised July 2022)

Remarks

(I)

The *Heart Sutra* (般若波羅蜜多心經) of Mahāyāna Buddhism (大乘佛教) is one of the most revered Buddhist sutras in China and Japan. The most widely known Chinese version of the *Heart Sutra* is the one arranged by Xuanzang (玄奘, 602-664 AD). The origin of the *Heart Sutra* is somewhat contentious, for some suggested that it was originally composed in Chinese but not in Sanskrit [8].

(II)

Xuanzang's version of the *Heart Sutra* is widely admired among traditional Chinese intellects and calligraphers. Ouyang Xun (歐陽詢, 557-641 AD) and Zhao Mengfu (趙孟頫, 1254-1322 AD) both scribed it in different script styles. Here, it is written in the small Standard Script (小楷).

(III)

The hand-scribing of Buddhist scriptures (or Sutra copying, or "抄經" in Chinese, or "写経" in Japanese) in the small standard script is relatively common in China and Japan. While some consider this practice a means of learning Buddhism, others consider it a meritorious act (功德), for it promotes the transmission and preservation of Buddhist scriptures.

Footnotes

(1) Collected in 《大正新脩大藏經》, p.848. Tokyo: 大藏出版株式會社, 1988 .

般若波羅蜜多心經 ❶

唐三藏法師玄 ❸ 奘譯

觀自在菩薩。行深般若波羅蜜多時。照見五蘊皆空。度一切苦厄。舍利子。色不異空。空不異色。色即是空。空即是色。受想行識亦復如是。舍利子。是諸法空相。不生不滅。不垢不淨。不增不減。是故空中。無色。無受想行識。無眼耳鼻舌身意。無色聲香味觸法。無眼界。乃至無意識界。無無明。亦無無明盡。乃至無老死。亦無老死盡。無苦集滅道。無智亦無得。以無所得故。菩提薩埵。依般若波羅蜜多故。心無罣礙。無罣礙故。無有恐怖。遠離顛倒夢想。究竟涅槃。三世諸佛。依般若波羅蜜多故。得阿耨多羅三藐三菩提。故知般若波羅蜜多。是大神咒。是大明咒。是無上咒。是無等等咒。能除一切苦。真實不虛故。說般若波羅蜜多咒即說咒曰 ❺

揭 ❹ 帝揭 ❺ 帝　般羅揭 ❻ 帝　般羅僧揭 ❺ 帝

菩提 ❼ 僧莎訶

般若波羅蜜多心經

(2). Conze, E., *Perfect Wisdom - The Short Prajñāpāramitā Texts*. Devon: Buddhist Publishing Group , 1973, pp.142-143.

(3). Ven. Dharma Master Lok To (Translator), Xuanzang, *The Prajna Paramita Heart Sutra*. New York : Sutra Translation Committee of the U.S. & Canada, 1995.

(4) "觀" here can take the meaning of "observing all with the mind (觀察人間)", while "自在" means "freely without restraint (自由自在)". See 馮炳基居士註釋,《般若波羅蜜多心經淺釋註解》. Hong Kong: Publisher unknown, 1993, pp.19-20.

(5) "行深" means "ruminated wisely and deeply". 馮炳基 elaborated: "智慧到彼岸, 不是口誦, 須是心行, 故曰行. 又非淺近之功, 故曰深." Ibid., p.20.

(6) While most translate "空" as "Void" or "Empty", it is more appropriate to translate it as "Nothingness". In Buddhism, "空" does not mean "void", "empty", or "non-existence (不存在)". Instead, it refers to the concept that all forms (色) of things, including con-

crete objects, phenomena, and abstract ideas, are ever-changing and thus in a state of "impermanence (無常)".

(7) "度" here means "transcend (出塵俗超生死)". See Taiwan's 中央研究院《搜詞尋字》online edition.

(8). Nattier, J., *The Heart Sutra: A Chinese Apocryphal Text?* See *The Journal of the International Association of Buddhist Studies*, vol.15, no.2, 1992, pp.153-223.

誠
Sincerity

明
Enlightenment

Great Learning

(《大學》)

Calligraphy

Calligrapher (書者): KS Vincent Poon (潘君尚)

Content (內容): *Great Learning* (《 大學 》)

Style (字體): Small Standard Script (小楷)

Caption (款識): 大學乃四書之一儒家之寶典也二零一九年己亥寒冬潘君尚書於多倫多尚尚齋 (The *Great Learning* is one of the Four Books and the canon of Confucian thoughts. The year of Two Thousand and Nineteen, during the freezing winter of the Jihai year. Scribed by KS Vincent Poon at The Senseis, Toronto)

Seal Inscription (鈐印): 君尚 (朱文) (Kwan Sheung, red characters), 潘氏 (白文) (The Surname of Poon, white characters)

Medium (材料): Ink on Xuan paper (紙墨水本)

Size (尺寸): 137 X 35cm each, 4 sheets

Year (年份): 2019

大學之道在明明德在親民在止於至善知止而后有定而后能靜靜而后能安安而后能慮慮而后能得物有本末事有終始知所先後則近道矣古之欲明明德於天下者先治其國欲治其國者先齊其家欲齊其家者先修其身欲修其身者先正其心欲正其心者先誠其意欲誠其意者先致其知致知在格物物格而后知至知至而后意誠意誠而后心正心正而后身修身修而后家齊家齊而后國治國治而后天下平自天子以至於庶人壹是皆以修身為本其本亂而末治者否矣其所厚者薄而其所薄者厚未之有也

康誥曰克明德大甲曰顧諟天之明命帝典曰克明峻德皆自明也

湯之盤銘曰苟日新日日新又日新康誥曰作新民詩曰周雖舊邦其命維新是故君子無所不用其極

詩云邦畿千里惟民所止詩云緡蠻黃鳥止于丘隅子曰於止知其所止可以人而不如鳥乎詩云穆穆文王於緝熙敬止為人君止於仁為人臣止於敬為人子止於孝為人父止於慈與國人交止於信

詩云瞻彼淇澳菉竹猗猗有斐君子如切如磋如琢如磨瑟兮僩兮赫兮喧兮有斐君子終不可諠兮如切如磋者道學也如琢如磨者自修也瑟兮僩兮者恂慄也赫兮喧兮者威儀也有斐君子終不可諠兮者道盛德至善民之不能忘也詩云於戲前王不忘君子賢其賢而親其

親小人樂其樂而利其利此以沒世不忘也

子曰聽訟吾猶人也必也使無訟乎無情者不得盡其辭大畏民志此謂

知本此謂知之至也 所謂誠其意者毋自欺也如惡惡臭如好好色此之謂自謙故君子必慎其獨也小

人閒居為不善無所不至見君子而后厭然揜其不善而著其善人之視己如見其肺肝然則何益矣此謂誠於中形於

外故君子必慎其獨也曾子曰十目所視十手所指其嚴乎富潤屋德潤身心廣體胖故君子必誠其意 所謂修身在

正其心者身有所忿懥則不得其正有所恐懼則不得其正有所好樂則不得其正有所憂患則不得其正心不在焉視

而不見聽而不聞食而不知其味此謂修身在正其心 所謂齊其家在修其身者人之其所親愛而辟焉之其所賤惡而

辟焉之其所畏敬而辟焉之其所哀矜而辟焉之其所敖惰而辟焉故好而知其惡惡而知其美者天下鮮矣故諺有

之曰人莫知其子之惡莫知其苗之碩此謂身不修不可以齊其家 所謂治國必先齊其家者其家不可教而能教人

者無之故君子不出家而成教於國孝者所以事君也弟者所以事長也慈者所以使眾也康誥曰如保赤子心誠求之

雖不中不遠矣未有學養子而后嫁者也一家仁一國興仁一家讓一國興讓一人貪戾一國作亂其機如此此謂一言

僨事一人定國堯舜帥天下以仁而民從之桀紂帥天下以暴而民從之其所令反其所好而民不從是故君子有諸己而后求諸人無諸己而后非諸人所藏乎身不恕而能喻諸人者未之有也故治國在齊其家詩云桃之夭夭其葉蓁蓁之子于歸宜其家人宜其家人而后可以教國人詩云宜兄宜弟宜兄宜弟而后可以教國人詩云其儀不忒正是四國其為父子兄弟足法而后民法之也此謂治國在齊其家所謂平天下在治其國者上老老而民興孝上長長而民興弟上恤孤而民不倍是以君子有絜矩之道也所惡於上毋以使下所惡於下毋以事上所惡於前毋以先後所惡於後毋以從前所惡於右毋以交於左所惡於左毋以交於右此之謂絜矩之道詩云樂只君子民之父母民之所好好之民之所惡惡之此之謂民之父母詩云節彼南山維石巖巖赫赫師尹民具爾瞻有國者不可以不慎辟則為天下僇矣詩云殷之未喪師克配上帝儀監于殷峻命不易道得眾則得國失眾則失國是故君子先慎乎德有德此有人有人此有土有土此有財有財此有用德者本也財者末也外本內末爭民施奪是故財聚則民散財散則民聚是故言悖而出者亦悖而入貨悖而入者亦悖而出康誥曰惟命不于常道善則得之不善則失之矣楚書曰楚國無以為寶惟

舅犯曰亡人無以為寶仁親以為寶秦誓曰若有一个臣斷斷兮無他技其心休休焉其如有容焉人之有技若己有之人之彥聖其心好之不啻若自其口出寔能容之以能保我子孫黎民尚亦有利哉人之有技媢疾以惡之人之彥聖而違之俾不通寔不能容以不能保我子孫黎民亦曰殆哉唯仁人放流之迸諸四夷不與同中國此謂唯仁人為能愛人能惡人見賢而不能舉舉而不能先命也見不善而不能退退而不能遠過也好人之所惡惡人之所好是謂拂人之性菑必逮夫身是故君子有大道必忠信以得之驕泰以失之生財有大道生之者眾食之者寡為之者疾用之者舒則財恆足矣仁者以財發身不仁者以身發財未有上好仁而下不好義者也未有好義其事不終者也未有府庫財非其財者也孟獻子曰畜馬乘不察於雞豚伐冰之家不畜牛羊百乘之家不畜聚斂之臣與其有聚斂之臣寧有盜臣此謂國不以利為利以義為利也長國家而務財用者必自小人矣彼為善之小人之使為國家菑害並至雖有善者亦無如之何矣此謂國不以利為利以義為利也

大學乃四書之一儒家之寶典也二零一九年己亥冬潘君尚喜於多倫多尚尚齋

Translation

The original classical Chinese of *Great Learning* and its text arrangement below follow Zhu Xi's (朱熹) venerable *Commentaries on the Four Books* (《四書集注》) [1]. Hence, the order of the paragraphs is slightly different than that seen in *Liji*'s (《 禮記 》).

This English translation amends numerous common misinterpretations in other English interpretations, including that by the revered James Legge[2] and two online renditions by A. Charles Mueller and Robert Eno[3]. With clear and concise language, it aims to facilitate a correct understanding of this foundational Confucian text.

《 大學 》
Great Learning

1. 大學之道，在明明德，在親民，在止於至善。
The Fundamental Way (道) of the Great Learning is to enlighten (明) one's inherent splendid virtue (明德), to revitalize (親,新)[4] the people, and to continuously pursue these endeavours until one rests and resides (止) in the highest level of excellence (至善).

2. 知止而后有定，定而后能靜，靜而后能安，安而后能慮，慮而后能得。
With knowing what to pursue and where to ultimately rest in, one then (后) has steadfast determination (定). With steadfast determination, one then can (能) be in a state of unmoved tranquillity (靜). With unmoved tranquillity, one then can be at ease (安) under any circumstance. With being at ease under any circumstance, one then can deliberate (慮) with great care. With deliberating with great care, one then can attain (得) the highest excellence.

3. 物有本末，事有終始，知所先後，則近道矣。
All things have their respective foundations (本) and ramifications (末); all affairs have their own conclusions (終) and beginnings (始). If one knows which comes before and which comes after, then one shall not be far from The Fundamental Way (道) of the Great Learning.

4. 古之欲明明德於天下者，先治其國；欲治其國者，先齊其家；欲齊其家者，先修其身；欲修其身者，先正其心；欲正其心者，先誠其意；欲誠其意者，先致其知，致知在格物。
Those in the past who wished (欲) to enlighten the inherent splendid virtues throughout (於) all under Heaven first governed (治) their states (國) well. Those who wished to govern their states well first brought good order (齊) to their families. Those who wished to bring good order to their own families first culti-

vated (修) their own selves. Those who wished to cultivate their own selves first brought about propriety (正) in their minds (心). Those who wished to bring about propriety (正) in their minds first developed honesty and sincerity (誠) in their thoughts (意). Those who wished to develop honesty and sincerity in their thoughts first pursued their knowledge (知) to the utmost degree (致). To pursue knowledge to the utmost degree lies in examing all matters and principles to the greatest extent (格物).

5. 物格而後知至，知至而後意誠，意誠而後心正，心正而後身修，身修而後家齊，家齊而後國治，國治而後天下平。
When all matters and principles have been examined to the greatest extent, then one's knowledge can be pursued to the utmost degree. When one's knowledge has been pursued to the utmost degree, then one's thoughts can develop honesty and sincerity. When one's thoughts have developed honesty and sincerity, then one can bring about propriety in one's mind. When one has brought about propriety in one's mind, then one can cultivate one's own self. When one has cultivated one's own self, then one can bring good order to one's own family. When one has brought good order to one's own family, then one can govern the state well. When one has governed the state well, one can then rule and settle all under Heaven.

6. 自天子以至於庶人，壹是皆以修身為本。其本亂而末治者否矣。其所厚者薄，而其所薄者厚，未之有也。此謂知本，此謂知之至也。
From the Son of Heaven to the ordinary layman, everyone (壹) takes the cultivation of oneself as one's foundation. For one to have a disorderly (亂) foundation yet end up (末) to govern well is not possible indeed (矣). What one considers very important (厚), yet one takes it lightly (薄); what one considers trivial (薄), yet one takes it with great importance (厚); such instances never existed. This is called knowing one's foundation; this is called pursuing knowledge to the utmost degree.

7. 《康誥》曰：「克明德。」《太甲》曰：「顧諟天之明命。」《帝典》曰：「克明峻德。」皆自明也。

Announcement to Kang (《康誥》) narrated, "capable (克) of enlightening one's inherent splendid virtue." *Tai Jia* (《太甲》) narrated, "always consider the Heavenly Decree (命) of enlightening one's inherent splendid virtue." *Canon of Emperor Yao* (《帝典》) narrated, "capable of enlightening one's great (峻) virtue." These all illustrate to self-enlighten one's inherent splendid virtue.

8. 湯之《盤銘》曰：「苟日新，日日新，又日新。」《康誥》曰：「作新民。」

These are the *Inscribed Words on the Washing Basin* (《盤銘》) of Emperor Tang (湯) of Shang: "if (苟) one can one day (日) revitalize (新) oneself, then one can revitalize oneself every single day (日日新) as well as (又) able to revitalize oneself on all other days (日新)." *Announcement to Kang* (《康誥》) narrated, "reinvigorate (作) and revitalize all people (民)."

9. 《詩》曰：「周雖舊邦，其命惟新。」是故君子無所不用其極。

The *Book of Odes* (《詩經》) narrated, "Despite Zhou was a state with a long history (before it replaced Shang), its acceptance of Heavenly decree (to replace Shang) is (惟) by revitalizing its people." Accordingly, the honourable ones pursue revitalizing themselves and others relentlessly with all possible means.

10. 《詩》云：「邦畿千里，惟民所止。」《詩》云：「緡蠻黃鳥，止于丘隅。」子曰：「於止，知其所止，可以人而不如鳥乎？」

The *Book of Odes* narrated, "The imperial capital domain (邦畿) of a thousand li (里) is wherein the people rest and reside (止, see Line 1)." The *Book of Odes* narrated, "The tweeting yellow birds rest and reside in the tranquil corners of a hill (丘隅)." Confucius once said, "Of (於) choosing wherein to rest and reside, even birds know wherein to rest and reside; how then can humankind not rival the birds?"

11. 《詩》云：「穆穆文王，於緝熙敬止！」為人君，止於仁；為人臣，止於敬；為人子，止於孝；為人父，止於慈；與國人交，止於信。

The *Book of Odes* narrated, "The deep and profound (穆穆) King Wen (文王) of Zhou, alas (於), continuously (緝) pursued enlightenment (熙) and paid great deference (敬) to where he should ultimately rest in!" As a sovereign, one should pursue and ultimately rest in being benevolent (仁). As a subordinate, one should pursue and ultimately rest in having deference (敬). As a son, one should pursue and ultimately rest in filial piety (孝). As a father, one should pursue and rest in being merciful and kind (慈). As a statesman who deals with all other people in the state, one should pursue and rest in being honest and trustworthy (信).

12. 《詩》云：「瞻彼淇澳，菉竹猗猗。有斐君子，如切如磋，如琢如磨。瑟兮僩兮，赫兮喧兮。有斐君子，終不可諠兮！」「如切如磋」者，道學也；「如琢如磨」者，自修也；「瑟兮僩兮」者，恂慄也；「赫兮喧兮」者，威儀也；「有斐君子，終不可諠兮」者，道盛德至善，民之不能忘也。

The *Book of Odes* narrated, "Look (瞻) at those (彼) banks of the river Qi (淇), the green (菉) bamboos are so luxuriant (猗猗). Brilliant (斐) honourable persons (君子) shine like they have been finely cut (切) and filed (磋) as well as chiselled (琢) and ground (磨). Solemn (瑟) indeed (兮), mighty (僩) indeed. Majestic (赫) indeed, distinguished (喧) indeed. Such honourable persons shall ultimately never be forgotten (諠)." The words "they are like those have been finely cut and filed" describe the attitudes of the honourable ones in walking the paths of learning. The words "they are like those who have been finely chiselled and ground" refer to the temperament of the honourable ones in cultivating themselves (自修). The words "solemn indeed, mighty indeed" describe the trembling fears (恂慄) of the honourable ones in their deliberations. The words "majestic indeed, distinguished indeed" describe the grand appearances (威儀) of the honourable ones. The words "brilliant and honourable persons shall ultimately never be forgotten" illustrate the rich abundance of virtues (盛

德) and impeccable goodness (至善) possessed by the honourable ones, and thus they are never forgotten by the people.

13. 《詩》云：「於戲前王不忘！」君子賢其賢而親其親，小人樂其樂而利其利，此以沒世不忘也。

The *Book of Odes* narrated, "Alas (於戲)! The former kings (前王, i.e. King Wen of Zhou, 周文王, and King Wu of Zhou, 周武王) are never forgotten." The honourable ones (君子) venerate those who they should venerate (賢其賢) and adore what they should adore (親其親). Dishonourable individuals (小人) merely seek delight in what delighted them (樂其樂) and pursue profits in whatever profited them (利其利). As such, even though the former kings have long perished from the world, they are never forgotten.

14. 子曰：「聽訟，吾猶人也，必也使無訟乎！」無情者不得盡其辭。大畏民志，此謂知本。

Confucius once said, "In hearing (聽) litigations (訟), I shall judge according to (猶)[5] to benevolence (人)[6], for this shall banish all litigations indeed!" Those without human nature (無情者, i.e., without benevolence and righteousness) will find it impossible to reach (盡) their arguments of litigation (辭). Such is the most venerable (大) awe that persuades (畏) the people's hearts (民志). This is called knowing the foundation (知本).

15. 此謂知本，此謂知之至也。

This is called knowing one's foundation[7]; this is called pursuing knowledge to the utmost degree.

16. 所謂誠其意者：毋自欺也，如惡惡臭，如好好色。此之謂自謙。故君子必慎其獨也！

The so-called "to develop honesty and sincerity in one's thoughts" is: not allowing oneself to be self-deceived (自欺), like one naturally dislikes bad smells (惡惡臭) or one loves beautiful entities (好好色). This is known as fulfilling (謙) oneself. As such, the honourable one is always more vigilant (慎) when alone (獨)!

17. 小人閒居為不善，無所不至。見君子而后厭然，揜其不善，而著其善。人之視己，如見其肺肝然，則何益矣。此謂誠於中，形於外，故君子必慎其獨也。

Dishonourable individuals, when they are alone (閒居), act with malevolence (不善) that reaches all corners without limits (無所不至). If they meet the honourable ones, they then (後) covertly (厭然) conceal (揜) their malevolence and show (著) everyone their goodwill and kindness. Yet, as people observe them, the people shall see right through them, as if seeing the very core of their minds (肺肝); how then can concealing be beneficial!? This is the so-called "the honesty residing in the core within always manifests (形) itself externally (外)"; as such, the honourable one is always more vigilant when alone!

18. 曾子曰：「十目所視，十手所指，其嚴乎！」

Zengzi once said, "Many, many eyes are always watching over you, and many many fingers are always pointing at you; how serious (嚴) indeed!"

19. 富潤屋，德潤身，心廣體胖，故君子必誠其意。

Wealth can adorn (潤) one's house, and virtues can adorn (潤) one's being. (If one is honest and sincere), one's mind shall be vast and magnanimous (廣), and one's body will be at ease (胖). Accordingly, the honourable ones must be honest and sincere in their thoughts.

20. 所謂脩身在正其心者，身有所忿懥，則不得其正；有所恐懼，則不得其正；有所好樂，則不得其正；有所憂患，則不得其正。心不在焉，視而不見，聽而不聞，食而不知其味。此謂脩身在正其心。

The so-called "cultivating the self resides in bringing about propriety in one's mind" is: if the mind (身 should be 心 here) holds anger and resentment (忿懥), then one cannot obtain propriety; if the mind holds fear (恐懼), then one cannot obtain propriety; if the mind indulges in delights (好樂), then one cannot obtain propriety;

if the mind is filled with apprehension (憂患), then one cannot obtain propriety. When the mind loses focus (在)[8], then one looks yet does not see, listens yet does not hear, eats yet does not know the taste. This is known as "cultivating the self resides in bringing about propriety in one's mind".

21. 所謂齊其家在脩其身者：人之其所親愛而辟焉，之其所賤惡而辟焉，之其所畏敬而辟焉，之其所哀矜而辟焉，之其所敖惰而辟焉。故好而知其惡，惡而知其美者，天下鮮矣！故諺有之曰：「人莫知其子之惡，莫知其苗之碩。」此謂身不脩不可以齊其家。

The so-called "to bring good order to one's family resides in cultivating the self" is: when people come into something they adore (親愛), they hold a bias (辟); when they come into something they abhor (賤惡), they hold a bias; when they come into something they revere (畏敬), they hold a bias; when they come into something that is sad and induces their pity (哀矜), they hold a bias. When they come into something that they deem as arrogant and lazy, they hold a bias. Accordingly, those who can find bad qualities in what they like and find good qualities in what they dislike are extremely rare (鮮) in the world indeed! Hence, there is a common saying: "One does not recognize the malevolence of one's son; one does not recognize the sprouts (苗) one raised have become robust (碩)". This is known as "if the self is not cultivated, then one cannot bring good order to one's family".

22. 所謂治國必先齊其家者：其家不可教而能教人者，無之。故君子不出家而成教於國。孝者，所以事君也；弟者，所以事長也；慈者，所以使眾也。《康誥》曰:「如保赤子。」心誠求之，雖不中不遠矣。未有學養子而后嫁者也！

The so-called "before governing the state well, one must first bring good order to one's family" is: one cannot cultivate one's family yet can cultivate others, such an instance does not exist. As such, the honourable ones do not leave their homes yet still can develop (成) the ways to cultivate the state. For those with filial piety (孝), they can serve their ruler; for those who pay respect to their elder brothers (弟), they can serve their superiors; for those who are merciful (慈) towards the juniors, they can administrate (使) the masses. *Announcement to Kang* (《康誥》) narrated, "Act as if you were rearing a newborn infant." If one sincerely (誠) looks for (求) the way to rear the infant, though one may not be precisely correct, one will not be far from being correct. No girl needs to learn and master the way of bringing up a child beforehand to thus get married!

23. 一家仁，一國興仁；一家讓，一國興讓；一人貪戾，一國作亂；其機如此。此謂一言僨事，一人定國。

If a family harbours benevolence, then the state shall be uplifted (興) towards having benevolence; if a family harbours courtesy and propriety (讓), then the state shall be uplifted towards having courtesy and propriety; if a ruler (人)[9] is greedy (貪) and cruel (戾), then the state shall move towards (作) chaos (亂). Such is the underlying root cause (機)[10] behind the dynamics of a state. This is known as "a single word can ruin (僨) a matter of concern (事), and a single ruler can settle (定) the entire state".

24. 堯舜帥天下以仁，而民從之；桀紂帥天下以暴，而民從之；其所令反其所好，而民不從。是故君子有諸己而后求諸人，無諸己而后非諸人。所藏乎身不恕，而能喻諸人者，未之有也。故治國在齊其家。

Yao and Shun led all under Heaven with benevolence, and so the people followed (從) them (之) to act with benevolence; Chieh and Chau led all under Heaven with brutality, and so the people followed them to act with brutality; if the ruler orders (令) others to act in contrary (反) to the ruler's personal inclinations (好), then the people shall never follow (從) the order. Hence, the honourable ones attain good qualities themselves first and then (而后) ask others to do the same; the honourable ones rid (無) themselves of bad qualities first and then ask others to rid the same. Not bearing "projecting oneself to reach all others (恕)"[11] yet can enlighten (喻)[12] other people, such an instance never existed. Hence, "governing the state well resides in bringing good order to one's family".

25.《詩》云：「桃之夭夭，其葉蓁蓁；之子于歸，宜其家人。」宜其家人，而后可以教國人。《詩》云：「宜兄宜弟。」宜兄宜弟，而后可以教國人。《詩》云：「其儀不忒，正是四國。」其為父子兄弟足法，而后民法之也。此謂治國在齊其家。

The *Book of Odes* narrated, "The peach blossoms, so pretty and sumptuous (夭夭)! How luxuriant is its foliage! When the girl marries into (于歸) her husband's household, she shall bring harmony (宜)[13] to her husband's family." When one has brought harmony to one's family, one can then cultivate the people of the state. The *Book of Odes* narrated, "Bring harmony among the elder and younger brothers." When one has brought harmony to one's elder and younger brothers, one can then cultivate the people of the state. The *Book of Odes* narrated, "When one's principle (儀) of being a decent person has not gone astray (忒), one can then bring propriety to all the states within the four corners of the Universe (四國, i.e., all under Heaven)[14]." If one's roles in being a father, a son, an elder brother, and a younger brother are all good enough (足) to be modelled (法), then the people shall take that as a model to follow. This is known as "governing the state resides in bringing good order to one's family".

26. 所謂平天下在治其國者：上老老而民興孝，上長長而民興弟，上恤孤而民不倍，是以君子有絜矩之道也。

The so-called "bringing peace to all under Heaven resides in governing one's state well" is: when the ruler (上) shows filial reverence to the elderly (老老), the people shall be uplifted (興) towards having filial piety (孝); when the ruler pays respect to the seniors (長長), the people shall be uplifted towards paying respect to the elderly brothers (弟); when the ruler shows compassion (恤) towards the weak and the underprivileged (孤), the people shall not turn their backs (倍) on the lonely and the disabled. Thus, the honourable ruler embraces the way (道) of such norms (絜)[15] and principles (矩)[16].

27. 所惡於上，毋以使下；所惡於下，毋以事上；所惡於前，毋以先後；所惡於後，毋以從前；所惡於右，毋以交於左；所惡於左，毋以交於右。此之謂絜矩之道。

What one dislikes in one's superiors, one should not apply it to treat one's subordinates; what one dislikes in one's subordinates, one should not apply it to serve one's superiors; what one dislikes in those who are in front, one should not apply it to lead (先) those who are behind; what one dislikes in those who are behind, one should not apply it to follow (從) those who are in front; what one dislikes to receive on the right, one should not bestow it upon the left; what one dislikes to receive on the left, one should not bestow it upon the right. Such is known as the way of norms and principles.

28. 《詩》云：「樂只君子，民之父母。」民之所好好之，民之所惡惡之，此之謂民之父母。

The *Book of Odes* narrated, "The honourable ones, who are agreeable and cheerful (樂只) with the people, are the parents of the people." When the ruler likes what the people like and dislikes what the people dislike, then the ruler can be called the parent of the people.

29. 《詩》云：「節彼南山，維石巖巖。赫赫師尹，民具爾瞻。」有國者不可以不慎，辟則為天下僇矣。

The *Book of Odes* narrated, "Lofty is that Southern Mountain, with its rugged masses of rocks! The mighty and solemn (赫赫) Imperial Mentor Yin (師尹), the people always watch and look up to you!" Those who take possession of the state cannot be indiscreet and negligent. If they choose to follow their own prejudice (辟) in governing, they will be slain (僇)[17] by all under Heaven indeed.

30. 《詩》云：「殷之未喪師，克配上帝；儀監于殷，峻命不易。」道得眾則得國，失眾則失國。

The *Book of Odes* narrated, "When the sovereigns of the Yin (殷) Dynasty had not yet lost (喪) the hearts and minds of the mass

(師), they were capable (克) of being compatible with the Supreme (上) Heaven (帝)[18]. One should (儀) thus carefully examine (監) the downfall of Yin. The Great (峻) Decree (命) from Heaven is not light and easy to carry (易)." This says (道) those who can attain the hearts and minds of the mass shall attain the state, while those who lose the hearts and minds of the mass shall lose the state.

31. 是故君子先慎乎德。有德此有人，有人此有土，有土此有財，有財此有用。德者本也，財者末也。外本內末，爭民施奪。是故財聚則民散，財散則民聚。是故言悖而出者，亦悖而入；貨悖而入者，亦悖而出。

As such, the honourable ones first pay great attention to their own virtues. Possessing good virtues shall then gain the hearts and minds of the people. Having the hearts and minds of the people shall then gain land. Having land shall then gain wealth. Having wealth shall then gain resources (用). Virtue is the foundation (本), while wealth is the consequential ramification (末, see Line 3). If a ruler neglects the foundation and weighs heavily on the ramification, then the ruler is competing with the people (爭民) and robbing (施奪) them. Therefore, if a ruler chooses to accumulate (聚) wealth, then the people shall leave and disperse away (散) from the state; if a ruler chooses to disperse wealth, then the people shall migrate and assemble (聚) towards the state. Hence, whoever delivers out (出) words (言) contrary to (悖) virtues shall receive words contrary to virtues; whatever is obtained by ways contrary to virtues shall be lost by ways contrary to virtues.

32. 《康誥》曰：「惟命不于常！」道善則得之，不善則失之矣。楚書曰：「楚國無以為寶，惟善以為寶。」舅犯曰：「亡人無以為寶，仁親以為寶。」

Announcement to Kang narrated, "Alas, the Heavenly Decree is not always with the ruler!" This says (道) those who are virtuous and kind (善) shall attain the Heavenly Decree, while those who are not virtuous and kind shall lose it. An ancient book from the state of Chu narrated, "Chu has nothing that can be treasured;

only its virtuousness and kindness are to be treasured." Uncle Fan (Zi Fan, 子犯, uncle of Duke Wen of Jin, 晉文公) said, "The Fugitive (Duke Wen of Jin) has nothing that can be treasured, only his benevolence and passion (仁親) are to be treasured."

33. 《秦誓》曰：「若有一个臣，斷斷兮無他技。其心休休焉，其如有容焉。 人之有技，若己有之；人之彥聖，其心好之，不啻若自其口出。寔能容之。 以能保我子孫黎民，尚亦有利哉。人之有技，媢疾以惡之；人之彥聖，而違之俾不通。 寔不能容。以不能保我子孫黎民，亦曰殆哉。」

The *Declaration of the Duke of Qin* narrated, "Suppose there is a minister who is plain and sincere (斷斷) but without any extraordinary talent. Nevertheless, this minister's mind is broad and accepting (休休) as well as full of tolerance and open-mindedness (有容). The talents of others, this minister regards them as if they were his own; virtuousness and wisdom of others, this minister cherishes (好) them in his mind and treat them as if (不啻) they are coming out of his lips. Such a minister is indeed (寔) capable of being tolerant and open-minded to all. This minister can thus protect my descendants and people as well as bring benefit to the state, certainly.

By contrast, the talents of others, this minister despises them with jealously; virtuousness and wisdom of others, this minister abandons (違) them and blocks their appointment. Such a minister is indeed incapable of being tolerant and open-minded to all. Thus, this minister cannot protect my descendants and people as well as bring peril to the state, certainly."

34. 唯仁人放流之，迸諸四夷，不與同中國。此謂唯仁人為能愛人，能惡人。

Only the benevolent person can send away and banish the malevolent ones, driving them out to the distant barbarous territories and determined not to dwell with them in the Central States (中國). This is known as called "only the benevolent person can love others and despise others."

35. 見賢而不能舉，舉而不能先，命也；見不善而不能退，退而不能遠，過也。好人之所惡，惡人之所好，是謂拂人之性，菑必逮夫身。

Seeing virtuous persons of great talent and not being able to endorse them to public office, or endorsing them but not being able to be close (先)[19] to them, negligence (命)[20] indeed. Seeing persons of wickedness and not being able to remove them, or removing them but not being able to stay away (遠) from them, moral mistakes (過) indeed. Like what others hate, and hate what others like; such is known as against (拂) the very nature of humans, and so calamities (菑) shall come down on him.

36. 是故君子有大道。必忠信以得之，驕泰以失之。生財有大道。生之者眾, 食之者寡; 為之者疾，用之者舒。則財恒足矣。

Thus, the honourable ones always embrace the "Great Principle (大道)". Being loyal to oneself (忠) and sincere to all (信) allows one to hold it; being conceited (驕) and arrogant (泰) leads one to lose it. Generating wealth and resources also has its own "Great Principle". Having many to generate with few to consume while having rapid production with slow consumption. Such shall make wealth and resources always sufficient.

37. 仁者以財發身，不仁者以身發財。未有上好仁, 而下不好義者也; 未有好義, 其事不終者也; 未有府庫財, 非其財者也。

The benevolent ones expend their wealth and resources to establish (發) their selves (身); the non-benevolent ones expend their selves to establish their wealth and resources. There has never been an instance where the ruler cherishes benevolence, yet the subjects do not cherish righteousness; there has never been an instance where the subjects cherish righteousness, yet the ruler's matters cannot be accomplished; there has never been an instance where the wealth in the treasuries are not the bona fide wealth of the ruler.

38. 孟獻子曰：「畜馬乘不察於雞豚，伐冰之家不畜牛羊，百乘之家不畜聚斂之臣。與其有聚斂之臣，寧有盜臣。」此謂國不以利為利，以義為利也。

Meng Xianzi once said, "Lower-class nobles, who retain horse carriages (畜馬乘), should not seek to benefit from ranching fowls and pigs; middle-class nobles, who chisel ice for their funerals (伐冰之家), should not pursue profits from raising cows and sheep; upper-class nobles, who possesses a hundred of carriages (百乘之家), should not cater a subordinate who amasses wealth from the people. Rather than holding such a subordinate who amasses wealth from the people, it is better for the lord to have a subordinate who robs himself." Such is known as "a state should never take any materialistic benefit as a bona fide benefit, it should always take righteousness as the bona fide benefit".

39. 長國家而務財用者，必自小人矣。 彼為善之。 小人之使為國家，災害并至。 雖有善者，亦無如之何矣！此謂國不以利為利，以義為利也。

Governing (長) a state to pursue (務) wealth and utility, the ruler must hence apply (自) those who are dishonourable. This is not (彼)[21] good (善). When the ruler applies the dishonourable ones to work for the state, calamities shall arise. Even in the presence of those who are honourable, nothing can be done! Such is known as "a state should never take any materialistic benefit as a bona fide benefit, and it should always take righteousness as the bona fide benefit".

(translated by KS Vincent Poon, Mar. 2021; revised July 2022)

Remarks

(I)

The *Great Learning* (《大學》) is a classical Confucian text that outlines the principles of being a well-educated person. It was written more than two thousand years ago and was named the first of the *Four Books* (四書) by the venerable Song Dynasty scholar Zhu Xi (朱熹, 1130-1200AD). During and after the Song Dynasty, the *Four Books* were always included in the standard curriculum for the Imperial Examination (科舉)[22], and so the *Great Learning* (《大學》) is one of the most studied texts in Chinese history.

(II)

Written in less than 2000 Chinese characters, the *Great Learning* first contends the ultimate outcome of academic excellence is the refinement of one's temperament (大學之道, 在明明德) as well as rejuvenating and enlightening others (在親民). It then details and justifies the essential elements in the pursuit of knowledge, such as being "honest (誠)" and avoiding personal "prejudices (辟)". The text concludes by scrutinizing governance in light of the principles outlined in the *Great Learning*.

(III)

In classical Chinese, "大學" should be interpreted as the "Great Learning to Refine One's Inherent Goodness and Brilliance"[23], not today's "University (大學)". Also, "小學", in classical Chinese, is "the study of writing and understanding basic Chinese characters", quite similar to today's linguistics[24]. "小學", in classical Chinese, is not today's "Elementary school (小學)". Those who study ancient Chinese education systems should pay great attention to these distinctions.

Footnotes

(1). 朱熹《四書集註》. Hong Kong: 太平書局 , 1968 , pp.1-15. And 蔣伯潛《語譯廣解大學讀本》, see 沈知方 主稿 《語譯廣解四書讀本》. Hong Kong: 啟明書局, publication year unknown.

(2). Legge, James, *Sacred Books of the East*, Vol.27, *The Li Ki*, edited by Max Mueller. Oxford: Clarendon Press , 1885.

(3). Mueller, A. Charles, *The Great Learning* . http://www.acmuller.net/con-dao/greatlearning.html. And Eno, Robert, *The Great Learning and The Doctrine of the Mean: Translation, Commentary, and Notes*. https://scholarworks.iu.edu/dspace/handle/2022/23422.

(4). "親" here actually means "新". "親, 又通作新", see *Kangxi Dictionary* (《康熙字典》).

An excellent example of equating "新" with "親" can be found in the *Book of Documents - Metal-bound Coffer* (《尚書•金縢》): "惟朕小子其新逆." See 孔安國《尚書孔傳•周書•金縢》. Taipei: 新興書局,1964, p.043. Jiang Boqian (蔣伯潛) contends " '親逆' 寫作'新逆', 正和 '新民' 寫作 '親民' 一樣 , 這是程朱讀 '親' 為 '新' 的一個有力旁証". See 蔣伯潛 《語譯廣解大學讀本》, as in footnote (1), p.2.

(5). "猶" here means "由 (according to)", as in:

    i.   "猶 , 借為由" in 《說文通訓定聲•孚部》.

    ii. In *Mencius - Gong Sun Chou I* (《孟子•公孫丑上》) : "尺地莫非其有也, 一民莫非其臣也, 然而文王猶方百里起, 是以難也." 朱熹注 : " '猶方'之 '猶' 與 '由' 通."

    Source: Taiwan's 中央研究院《搜詞尋字》online edition.

(6). "人" here is "仁 (benevolence)", as in:

    i.   《呂氏春秋•舉難》 : "故君子責人則以人, 責己則以義."俞樾平議：下人字當讀作仁. 責人則以仁, 與下文自責則以義正相對."
ii.　《穀梁傳•莊公元年》：接練時, 錄母之變, 始人之也."王引之述
聞："人之者, 仁之也."
Source: Taiwan's 中央研究院《搜詞尋字》online edition.

(7) Repetitive phrase according to Cheng Yi, "程子曰：衍文也". See 朱熹《四書集註•大學》,as in footnote (1), p.5.

(8). "在" here means "to observe/focus (省視/觀察)", as in:

i.　"在,察也" in *Erya - Shigu II* (《爾雅•釋詁下》). 郭璞, 《爾雅郭注》Volume 1, 釋詁下, p.19b. Taipei: 新興書局, 1964, p.012.
ii.　In the *Book of Documents - Canon of Shun* (《尚書•舜典》): "在璿璣玉衡, 以齊七政." 孔傳: "在, 察也." See 孔安國《尚書孔傳 •虞書 • 舜典》, as in footnote (4), p.006.

(9). "人" here means "ruler (君)", as annotated by Zhu Xi (朱熹): "一人, 謂君也." See 朱熹《四書集註•大學》, as in footnote (1), p.9.

(10). "機" here means "underlying root cause (發動所由)", as annotated by Zhu Xi (朱熹): "機, 發動所由也." Ibid..

(11). "恕" means "projecting oneself to reach all others (推己以及人)", as annotated by Zhu Xi (朱熹): "皆推己以及人，所謂恕也." Ibid..

(12). "喻" here means "enlighten (曉)", accordingly to *Yupian* (《玉篇•口部》). See Taiwan's 中央研究院《搜詞尋字》online edition.

(13). "宜" here means "和順 (bring harmony)". In the *Book of Odes - Odes Of Zhou And The South* (《詩經•周南》): "之子于歸、宜其室家." See 朱熹 《詩經集註》. Hong Kong: 廣智書局, publication year unknown, p.4. According to *Kangxi Dictionary* (《康熙字典》), "宜其室家, 宜者, 和順之意."

(14). "四國" here means "all under Heaven (天下)", as seen in the *Book of Odes - Greater Odes of the Kingdom - Song Gao* (《詩經•大雅•崧高》): "揉此萬邦，聞于四國." See 朱熹 《詩經集註》, as above, p.167. In 《漢語大詞典》, "四方鄰國，泛指天下." 上海: 上海辭書出版社, 2008, p.589.

(15). "絜" here means "rules and norms (尺/度)", as annotated by Zhu Xi (朱熹): "絜, 度也." See 朱熹《四書集註•大學》, as in footnote (1), p.10.

(16). "矩" here means "principles (方/法度)", as annotated by Zhu Xi (朱熹): "矩, 所以為方也." Ibid..

(17). "僇" here means "戮 (slain)", as annotated by Zhu Xi (朱熹): "僇, 同戮." Ibid., p.11.

(18). "帝" here means "Heaven (天)", as in:

i.   "帝青九萬里, 空洞無一物" in Wang Anshi's (王安石) *Gu Yi* (《古意》). See Taiwan's 中央研究院 《搜詞尋字》 online edition.

ii.   In the *Book of Documents - Yao Dian* (《書經•堯典》) : "昔在帝堯, 聰明文思, 光宅天下." See 孔安國《尚書孔傳 •虞書 • 堯典》, as in footnote (4), p. 004. In *Kangxi Dictionary* (《康熙字典》), "帝者, 天之一名, 所以名帝."

(19). "先" here is "be close to (近)", as annotated by Jiang Boqian (蔣伯潛) :

俞樾 《羣經平議》 說: " '先' 蓋 '近' 字之誤. '見賢而不能舉, 舉而不能近' 與 '見不善而不能退, 退而不能遠' 正相對成文."
Source: 蔣伯潛 《語譯廣解大學讀本》, as in footnote (1), p.22.

(20). "命" here means "negligence (怠慢)", as annotated by Zhu Xi (朱熹): " 命，鄭氏云 '當作慢'. 程子云 '當作怠'. " See 朱熹《四書集註•大學》, as in footnote (1), p.13.

(21) "彼" is "匪 ", which means "非 (not)", accordingly to *Shuowen*

Tongxun Dingsheng (《說文通訓定聲》): "彼, 借為匪, 實為非."
See Taiwan's 中央研究院 《搜詞尋字》 online edition.

(22). The Imperial Examination (科舉) was implemented in various dynasties for the selection of officers.

(23). "大學", in classical Chinese, means ""Great Learning to Refine One's Inherent Goodness and Brilliance". According to Jiang Boqian (蔣伯潛), " '大學之道', 就是養成此種充實而有光輝的理想的人格之修養方法." See 蔣伯潛《語譯廣解大學讀本》, as in footnote (1), p.2.

(24). "小學", in classical Chinese, is the study of writing and understanding basic Chinese characters. Taiwan's 教育部《重編國語辭典修訂本》online edition: "小學, 研究文字字形、字義及字音的學問. 包括文字學、聲韻學及訓詁學."

Revisions to "An English Translation and the Correct Interpretation of Laozi's Tao Te Ching"

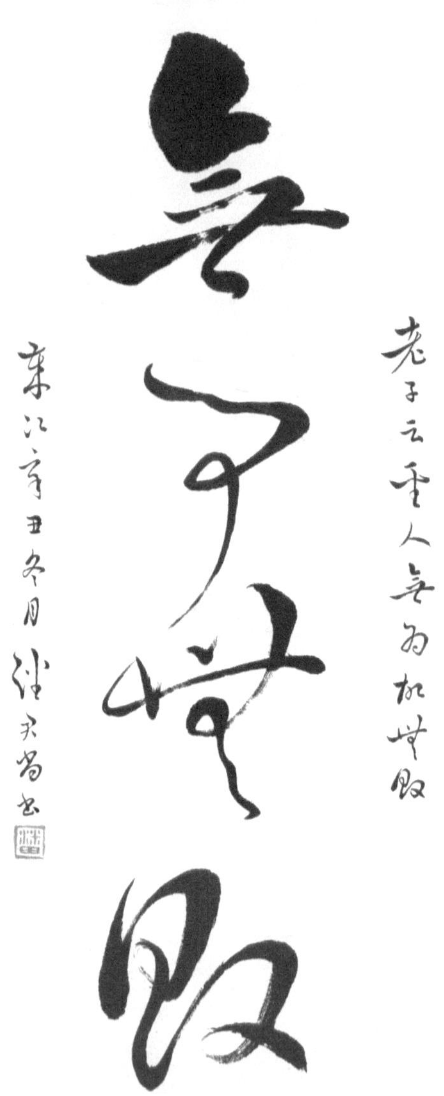

If one does not pursue personal feats, one shall never face defeat
無事無敗
Cursive Script 69 X 33 cm
KS Vincent Poon 2022

Revisions to "An English Translation and the Correct Interpretation of Laozi's Tao Te Ching"

KS Vincent POON (潘君尚) & Kwok Kin POON (潘國鍵)

This document outlines 15 revisions to our book, *An English Translation and the Correct Interpretation of Laozi's Tao Te Ching* (英譯並正解老子道德經, Toronto: The SenSeis, 2020). The numbers at the beginning of the original Chinese text are identical to those found in the book.

<u>Revisions are represented by the underlined texts.</u>

69. 希言自然。故飄風不終朝, 驟雨不終日。孰為此者 ? 天地。天地尚不能久, 而況於人乎!
<u>The words (言) from Tao's fundamental nature (自然) are the tranquilities that can never be heard (希)</u>. Therefore, sounds from violent winds (飄風) do not last from <u>one morning to the other (朝)</u>, and noises from sudden torrential rains (驟雨) do not last for an entire day. What directs all these? The Universe. Even the Universe cannot make its own act last forever, let alone (況於) mere humans!

105. 柔弱勝剛強。魚不可脫於淵。國之利器不可以示人。
The gentle and weak is better than (勝) the bold and strong. <u>A lively fish</u> should not leave its <u>soothing and abyssal niche (淵)</u>. <u>Mighty and powerful</u> instruments that benefit the state (國之利器) should not be displayed to the people.

112. 昔之得一者 : 天得一以清; 地得一以寧; 神得一以靈; 谷得一以盈; 萬物得一以生; 侯王得一以為天下貞。其致之。
Those that have obtained One since the past are: Nature, which carries One to become pure and clear (清); Earth, which carries One to become settled and established (寧); the spirits, which carry One to obtain their vitalities (靈); the valleys (谷), which

carry One to become filled with abundant diversity (盈); all things, which carry One to live and exist (生); the rulers (侯王) of states, <u>who carry One to become the heads (貞)</u>[1] <u>of states</u>. The One (其) fulfils and realizes (致) all their corresponding characteristics (之).

Note (1): "貞" is "正 (govern)". See《易經•乾卦》"元亨利貞" (Zhengzhou: 中州古籍出版社, 1993, p.1) ,"貞, 正也" (citing《周易正義》in the same book, p.2). And "正" is "長 (head/governor)". See 《爾雅•釋詁》,"正，長也"(郭璞,《爾雅郭注》Volume 1, 釋詁下, p.17a. Taipei: 新興書局, 1964, p.011). Thus "貞" should be "heads of states (君長)".

116. 上士聞道, 勤而行之; 中士聞道, 若存若亡; 下士聞道, 大笑之。不笑不足以為道。

<u>Those of the highest calibre (上士)</u>, when they hear about (聞) Tao, earnestly (勤) act according to it. <u>Those of the average calibre (中士)</u>, when they hear about Tao, sometimes keep (存) it and sometimes lose (亡) it. <u>Those of the lowest calibre (下士)</u>, when they hear about Tao, laugh greatly at it; if it were not laughed at by them, it would not be fit to be Tao.

119. 道生一; 一生二; 二生三; 三生萬物。萬物負陰而抱陽, 沖氣以為和。

Tao spawned (生) One; One spawned Two; Two spawned Three; Three spawned all things. All things possess the negative (陰, Yin) and embrace the positive (陽, Yang), and the interactions (沖) between these two countering forces (氣) make all things <u>cohesive in harmony (和)</u>.

136. 聖人在天下, 歙歙為天下渾其心。聖人皆孩之。

The wise sages living under Heaven have no prejudice (歙歙) of their own and turn the minds (心) of all under Heaven back to their primitive simplistic natures (渾). <u>The wise sages make all revert back to the states of being newborn babies (孩)</u>.

139. 道生之, 德畜之; 物形之, 勢成之。是以萬物莫不尊道而貴德。
Tao begets (生) all things, the Manifestation of Tao nurtures (畜) all things. <u>Tao applies shapes and forms (物) to exhibit (形) all things and uses styles and manners (勢) to establish all things.</u> Therefore, all things honour Tao and exalt its Manifestation.

140. 道之尊, 德之貴, 夫莫之命而常自然。故道生之, 德畜之; 長之育之, 亭之毒之; 養之覆之。生而不有, 為而不恃, 長而不宰。是謂玄德。
Although Tao should be honoured and its Manifestation exalted, all things do not need to be directed (命) by them to <u>invariably (常) follow Tao's own nature (自然).</u> Tao begets (生) all, and its Manifestation nurtures (畜) all; they both rear (長) all, raise (育) all, cultivate (亭) all, develop (毒) all, feed (養) all, and return (覆) all back to Tao. Tao begets all without anything (不有), acts without relying (不恃) on any other, and oversees (長) all without dominating (宰) over them. Such is known as the "Most Mysterious Manifestation of Tao (玄德)".

176. 古之善為道者, 非以明民, 將以愚之。民之難治, 以其智多。故以智治國, 國之賊; 不以智治國, 國之福。知此兩者亦稽式。
Those in the past who are well-acquainted (善) with Tao act not to make the people more intelligent (明) but rather to make them less intelligent. The people become difficult to govern because (以) they have too much acquired intelligence (智). Those who use acquired intelligence to govern are vandals (賊) to the state, while those who do not are blessings (福) to the state. <u>Governing (知)[2] both these cases is the same (稽) law (式) that follows Tao.</u>

Note (2): "知" here means "主 (to oversee)". See 《易經•繫辭》「乾知大始」(As in note (1), p.223), and 《左傳•襄公二十六年》「公孫揮曰：子產其將知政矣」(《左傳白話譯註》, Shang-hai: 上海書店, 1985, p.913). Thus, "知" can take the meaning of "to oversee (主)", and it is here interpreted as "to govern (掌管)".

177. 常知稽式, 是謂玄德。玄德深矣, 遠矣, 與物反矣, 然後乃至大順。

<u>This unchanging and everlasting Tao (常) governing (知) with the same law (稽式) in all cases is known as the "Most Mysterious Manifestation of Tao (玄德)".</u> This "Most Mysterious Manifestation of Tao" is so deep (深) and far-reaching (遠) indeed that it engages (與) in reverting (反) all worldly matters to their respective inherent simplicities. Eventually (然後), all then (乃) shall reach (至) to the "Great Conformity to Tao (大順)".

182. 我有三寶, 持而保之: 一曰慈, 二曰儉, 三曰不敢為天下先。慈故能勇; 儉故能廣; 不敢為天下先, 故能成器長。

I have three treasures (三寶) that I always uphold (持) and rely on (保): the first is earnest adoration (慈) of Tao, the second is frugality (儉), and the third is not daring to lead and be the most preeminent (先) among all under Heaven. When one adores Tao, one can thus be courageous (勇); when one is frugal, one can thus flourish (廣); when one dares not to lead and be the most preeminent among all under Heaven, one can thus become (成) <u>a venerable and agreeable (器) leader (長) among all.</u>

185. 是謂不爭之德, 是謂用人之力, 是謂配天古之極。

Such is known as the attainment (德) of being not competitive, the genuine way to unleash the true capabilities (力) of one's subordinates, and being compatible (配) with the pinnacle (極) of the <u>laws (古)</u>[3] of Nature (天).

Note (3): "古" here is "故". See 《爾雅郭注》 「古, 故也」 (As in note (1), p11a, p.008). "故" is "laws (事理/法則)". See 《易經•繫辭》 "仰以觀於天文, 俯以察於地理, 是故知幽明之故" (As in note (1), p. 225). Thus, "古" can be interpreted as "laws". As such, "天古" here refers to "laws of Nature."

208. 孰能有餘以奉天下, 唯有道者! 是以聖人為而不恃, 功成而不處。其不欲見賢。

Who then can take from the abundant to gift (奉) to all under

Heaven? Only Tao, of course (者)! Hence, wise sages act without relying on others (不恃) and accomplish without claiming any credit. <u>They never wish to show (見) any talent (賢) to anyone.</u>

217. 信言不美, 美言不信; 善者不辯, 辯者不善; 知者不博, 博者不知。

True and honest words (信言) are never nice, while nice words are never true and honest. Those who are well acquainted (善) with Tao <u>do not embellish their words (辯)</u>, while those who <u>embellish their words</u> are not well acquainted with Tao. Those who understand (知) Tao do not understand a wide range (博) of acquired knowledge, while those who understand a wide range of acquired knowledge do not understand Tao.

As for footnote (108) of the book annotating"新":

(108) "新" here actually means "親". "親, 又通作新", see *Kangxi Dictionary* (《康熙字典》).

<u>An excellent example of equating "新" with "親" can be found in the *Book of Documents - Metal-bound Coffer* (《尚書•金滕》): "惟朕小子其新逆." See 孔安國《尚書孔傳•周書•金滕》. Taipei: 新興書局,1964, p.043. Jiang Boqian (蔣伯潛) further contends:</u>

<u>"尚書金滕篇，成王說：'惟朕小子其新逆.' 成王這句話是說要親自迎接周公. '親逆' 寫作'新逆'，正和 '新民' 寫作 '親民' 一樣，這是程朱讀 '親' 為 '新' 的一個有力旁証. 新是去舊維新的意思; '新民' 是使人人能去其舊染之污, '日日新、又日新' 地振作起來."</u>
<u>Source: 蔣伯潛,《語譯廣解大學讀本》, see 沈知方主稿 《語譯廣解四書讀本》. Hong Kong: 香港啟明書局, publication year unknown, p. 2.</u>

July 2022

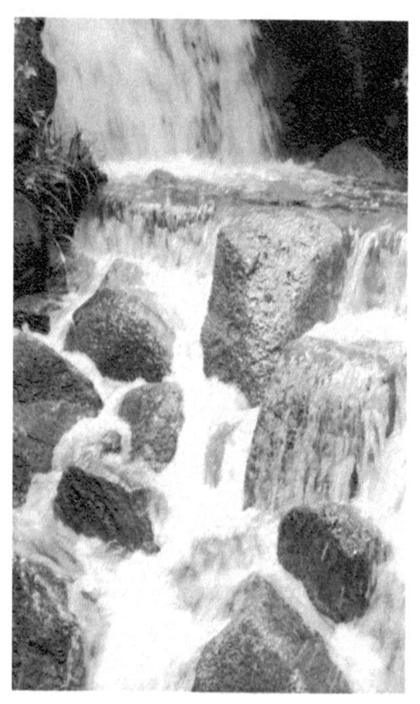

Tokugawa Garden
徳川園
Nagoya Japan
Photographed by KS Vincent Poon
2018

Zhuangzi - The Secret of Caring for Life

(《莊子•養生主》)

Calligraphy

Calligrapher (書者): KS Vincent Poon (潘君尚)

Content (內容): *Zhuangzi - The Secret of Caring for Life* (《莊子•養生主》)

Style (字體): Standard Script (楷書)

Caption (款識): 莊子養生主壬寅潘君尚書(*Zhuangzi - The Secret of Caring for Life,* year of the Renyin, scribed by KS Vincent)

Seal Inscription (鈐印): 潘 (朱文) (Poon, red character), 君尚 (白文) (Kwan Sheung, white characters)

Medium (材料): Ink on Xuan paper (紙墨水本)

Size (尺寸): 64 X 35cm

Year (年份): 2022

吾生也有涯而知也无涯以有涯隨无涯殆已已而為知者殆而已矣為善无近名為惡无近刑緣督以為經可以保身可以全生可以養親可以盡年

莊子養生主 壬寅潘君尚書

Translation

Note: *Please see Remarks (III) for some elaborations.*

《莊子•養生主》
Zhuangzi - The Secret of Caring for Life

1. 吾生也有涯，而知也无涯。以有涯隨无涯，殆已。
Our lives are limited, yet "intelligence and knowledge (知)" is unlimited. Applying the limited to pursue the unlimited, perilous (殆) indeed.

2. 已而為知者，殆而已矣。
Knowing this and still desire to become an "intelligent and knowledgeable person (知者)", perilous surely indeed (而已矣).

3. 為善无近名，為惡无近刑。
Being so-called "good (善)" shall not bring oneself to stick closely (近)[1] to any fame (名), being so-called "bad (惡)" shall not bring oneself to stick closely to any tragedy (刑)[2].

4. 緣督以為經，
By following (緣) what is the "Most Central of All Things (督)[3]" as the way (經)[4] of living,

5. 可以保身，可以全生，可以養親，可以盡年。
one can protect one's body, one can preserve one's life, one can nourish one's physical and mental self (親)[5], and one can live one's natural term of life to the fullest extent.

(translated by KS Vincent Poon, Mar. 2021; revised July 2022)

Remarks

(I)

Zhuangzi (《莊子》) is a canonical text of Taoism (道家) presumably written by Zhuang Zhou (莊周), a Chinese philosopher of the 4th Century BC. Zhuang Zhou, courtesy name Zixiu (子休) and commonly known today as Zhuangzi (莊子), was a care-free and independent man who was always at ease and held himself in high regard[6]. He even rejected invitations from the rulers of Qi (齊) and Chu (楚) to become their ministers[7]. His philosophy adhered mainly to that of Laozi's (老子), and he devoted many words to his own views on the Universe[8, 9]. Zhuangzi largely outlines his thoughts in *Zhuangzi* of about thirty-three chapters[10] and, along with Laozi's *Tao Te Ching* (《道德經》), is considered to be one of the two foundational texts of Taoism (道家).

(II)

The calligraphy presented is the introductory paragraph of *Zhuangzhi*'s chapter *The Secret of Caring for Life* (or *Nourishing the Lord of Life*, 《養生主》)[11]. The *Secret of Caring for Life* deliberates on the importance of following and obeying Tao (道) in maintaining and living one's natural term of life to the fullest extent.

(III)

Although this introductory paragraph is short, it succinctly outlines many philosophical concepts of Laozi.

(a)

以有涯隨无涯，殆已。
Applying the limited to pursue the unlimited, perilous indeed.

Zhuangzi's narration on the "limit (涯)" here is an elaboration on "where to reach and when to stop (止)" in Laozi's *Tao Te Ching* (《道德經》):

i. 《道德經》 第三十二章
「始制有名。名亦既有，夫亦將知止。知止可以不殆。」
Tao Te Ching Chapter 32
"The Originator manifests and generates the 'identifiable and with names'. Since the Name is already identifiable and thus limited, one should know where to reach and when to stop. Knowing where to reach and when to stop shall allow one to be free from all peril." [12]

ii. 《道德經》 第四十四章
「知足不辱; 知止不殆; 可以長久。」
Tao Te Ching Chapter 44
"Knowing to be satisfied with whatever the circumstances shall never bring shame to oneself; while knowing where to reach and when to stop shall never bring peril to oneself. Able to do both shall make one live long." [13]

(b)

已而為知者，殆而已矣。
Knowing this and still desire to become an 'intelligent and knowledgeable person', perilous surely indeed.

Here, the deliberation on being "intelligent and knowledgable (知)" is an extension to *Tao Te Ching*'s (《道德經》) depictions of the detriments of acquiring intelligence or knowledge:

i. 《道德經》 第十八章
「慧智出, 有大偽。」

Tao Te Ching Chapter 18
"When acquired wisdom and intellect come about, great hypocrisy appears." [14]

ii. 《道德經》第十九章
「絕聖棄智, 民利百倍。」
Tao Te Ching Chapter 19
"If a society abandons living by the examples of the so-called sages as well as leaving behind acquired wisdom, then its people will benefit a hundredfold." [15]

iii.《道德經》 第二十章
「絕學無憂。」
Tao Te Ching Chapter 20
"If one insulates oneself from acquiring knowledge and not follow scholarly disciplines, then one shall be free from worries." [16]

iv. 《道德經》第六十五章
「民之難治, 以其智多。」
Tao Te Ching Chapter 65
"The people become difficult to govern because they have too much acquired intelligence." [17]

(c)

為善无近名 , 為惡无近刑。
Being so-called 'good' shall not bring oneself to stick closely to any fame, being so-called 'bad' shall not bring oneself to stick closely to any tragedy.

Tao, the Way of the Universe, does not operate by the human-imposed concept of "good (善)" and "bad (惡)", for the Universe treats all things with no mercy, as described in Laozi's *Tao Te Ching* (《道德經》) :

《道德經》第五章
「天地不仁, 以萬物為芻狗; 聖人不仁, 以百姓為芻狗。」
Tao Te Ching Chapter 5

"The Universe does not follow the concept of being benevolent. It treats all things with no mercy as if they are straw-made dogs." [18]

Laozi in *Tao Te Ching* (《道德經》) further argued, rhetorically, that there is no difference between the so-called "good" and "bad":

《道德經》第二十章
「善之與惡, 相去若何？」
Tao Te Ching Chapter 20
"What is defined as 'good' and what is defined as 'bad', how different are they?" [19]

Thus, for followers of Tao, there is no such thing as being "good" nor being "bad". They simply follow the way of the Universe, the Great Tao. As such, they do not regard anything as "fame" nor "tragedy". Hence, Laozi wrote in *Tao Te Ching* (《道德經》):

《道德經》 第五十八章
「禍兮福之所倚, 福兮禍之所伏。孰知其極？ 其無正!」
Tao Te Ching Chapter 58
"Tragedies indeed have good fortunes sitting next to them, while good fortunes indeed have tragedies lurking beneath them. Who knows which one is the actual ultimate? Tao itself does not have any so-called agreeable sides!" [20]

Ge Hong's (葛洪) *Baopuzi* (《抱朴子》) further elaborated on this philosophy: "The wise do not necessarily live long, the dim-witted do not necessarily live short; 'good' does not stick closely to fortune, 'bad' does not stick closely to tragedy (賢不必壽，愚不必夭 ；善無近福，惡無近禍)." See *Baopuzi - Inner Chapters - Sainan* (《抱朴子•內篇 •塞難》).

(d)

可以養親 。

One can nourish one's physical and mental self.

"養親" usually means "supporting/looking after one's parents" in a variety of Confucian texts. However, it cannot take this meaning here, for Laozi rejects all human-imposed values, including Confucian "filial piety (孝)".

Since "保身", "全生", and "盡年", all relate to the personal self, relating "養親" here to one's parents, like Legge's rendition[21], is thus illogical.

"保身", "全生", "盡年", and "養親" are all enjoyed personally by "those who are well acquainted with maintaining their lives (善攝生者)" in Chapter 50 of Laozi's *Tao Te Ching*, for these people "never put themselves in dire and deadly situations (以其無死地)"[22].

Footnotes

(1) "近" here means "close to the extreme (切近)", as indicated in 《詩•周南•關雎序》："故正得失，動天地，感鬼神，莫近于詩. 孔穎達疏：無有近於詩者，言詩最近之，餘事莫之先也." See Taiwan's 中央研究院《搜詞尋字》online edition. "近" here is thus translated as "stick closely to".

(2) "刑" here is better interpreted as "tragedy (災害)" to contrast the favourable "fame (名)", as indicated in:

    i. 《國語•越語下》："天地未形，而先為之征，其事是以不成，雜受其刑. 韋昭注：刑，害也."
    ii. 《列子•楊朱》："從性而游，不逆萬物所好；死後之名非所取也，故不為刑所及. 殷敬順釋文：刑，害也."
    Source: Taiwan's 中央研究院《搜詞尋字》online edition.

(3) "督" here is "Central (中)", as annotated by Cheng Xuanying (成玄英) regarding this sentence. See 郭慶藩《莊子集釋》. Beijing: 中華書局, 1985, p.117. This is also suggested by:

    i. 《字彙•目部》："督，中也."
    ii. 《太玄•周》："植中樞，立督慮也. 司馬光注：督，猶中也."
    Source: 中央研究院《搜詞尋字》, ibid..

"中" here is "Central", which is Tao, the "original intrinsic idle tranquillity". As in Chapter 5 of *Tao Te Ching* (《道德經》), "Speaking too much invariably results in the loss of all arguments; hence, it is better to follow and keep one's original idle tranquillity (多言數窮, 不如守中)", Wang Chunfu (王純甫) annotated:

    中也者, 中也, 虛也, 無也, 不可言且名者也.
    "中" here means Central, Idle, Void, and Cannot Be Spoken nor Named.
    Source: KS Vincent Poon & Kwok Kin Poon, *An English Translation and the Correct Interpretation of Laozi's Tao Te Ching*. Toronto: The SenSeis, 2020, p.18.

Accordingly, in annotating "緣督以為經", Cheng Xuanying (成玄英) recommended all to forget the concept of "good" and "bad" and thus reside in the most central and important Tao:

夫善惡兩忘，刑名雙遣，故能順一中之道.
Source: 郭慶藩《莊子集釋》, as in footnote (3), p.116.

(4) "經" here should be better interpreted as "way/path (徑)" rather than "invariable law/what is constant (常)" seen in other interpretations. This is because *The Secret of Caring for Life* (《養生主》) narrates what path one should take to preserve one's life.

"經" can take the meaning of "way/path (徑)", as indicated in *Kangxi Dictionary* (《康熙字典》):

i. 《離騷》 王逸註: "經，徑也."
ii. 《釋名》:"經，徑也。如徑路無所不通，可常用也."

(5) "親" here is "self (自)", as suggested in:

i. 《禮•文王世子》 ："世子親齊而養. 註: 親，猶自也." See *Kangxi Dictionary* (《康熙字典》).
ii. 《詩•小雅•節南山》 ："弗躬弗親，庶民弗信." See 朱熹 《詩經集註》. Hong Kong: 廣智書局, publication year unknown, p.101.

(6) 陸德明: "(莊子)獨高尚其事, 優遊自得." See 郭慶藩,《莊子集釋》, as in footnote (3), p.4.

(7) 陸德明: "齊楚嘗聘以(莊子)為相, 不應." Ibid..

(8) 陸德明: "(莊子)依老氏之旨, 著書十餘萬言，以逍遙自然無為齊物而已." Ibid..

(9) "莊子哲學中之道德二觀, 與老子同." See 馮友蘭,《中國哲學小史》. Hong Kong: 文瀚出版社, 1969, p.37.

(10) 郭慶藩,《莊子集釋》. As in footnote (3), pp.4-5.

(11) Burton Watson translated 《養生主》 as *The Secret of Caring for Life* , while James Legge translated it as *Nourishing the Lord of Life*. See Burton Watson, *The Complete Works of Chuang Tzu*. New York: Columbia University Press, 1968. Also, Jame Legge, *Sacred Books of the East, The Texts of Taoism*, edited by Max Mueller. Oxford: Clarendon Press , 1891.

(12) KS Vincent Poon & Kwok Kin Poon, *An English Translation and the Correct Interpretation of Laozi's Tao Te Ching*, as in footnote (3), p.37.

(13) Ibid., p.47.

(14) Ibid., p.27.

(15) Ibid.

(16) Ibid., p.28.

(17) Ibid., p.62.

(18) Ibid., p.18.

(19) Ibid., p.28.

(20) Ibid., p.56.

(21) Jame Legge , as in footnotes (11).

(22) KS Vincent Poon & Kwok Kin Poon, *An English Translation and the Correct Interpretation of Laozi's Tao Te Ching*, as in footnote (3), p. 50.

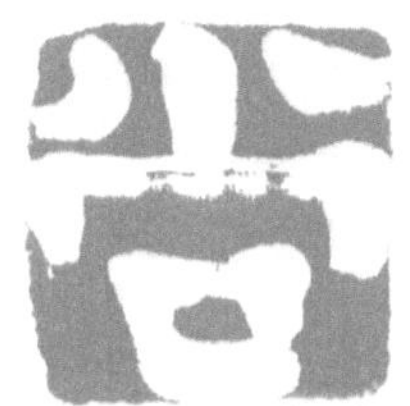

The SenSeis